Letters Home,
The Ohio Veterans Plaza

compiled by

Daniel A. Meeks

and

David E. Aldstadt

Veterans For Youth Foundation is a non-profit
organization that is dedicated to helping the nations
youth experience all the joys and freedoms this nation's
veterans served, sacrificed and died to protect.

Dear Reader,

       "Letters Home, The Ohio Veterans Plaza" is a collection of letters submitted to the state of Ohio, by the citizens of Ohio, to pay tribute to the men and women who have served our country. While reading this collection you may feel certain emotions that a solider experiences while being separated from family and friends. It is our hope that those emotions you may experience, love, despair, fear, anger, and others, will give you a brief look at how a solider feels and what a tremendous burden we place upon the families that send their loved ones off to protect our way of life. This is just a small sample of what those who protect us must endure.

       The last names of the sender and the receiver have been omitted to protect the privacy of the families. We wish to thank those families for opening their hearts and memories so that future generations can experience the otherwise unknown and unheralded cost of freedom paid by those that served to defend it and by those waiting for the defenders to return.

       With great respect and admiration,

       Daniel A. Meeks and David E. Aldstadt

SPECIAL THANKS to my son, Daniel A. Meeks Jr. who spent many hours helping compile the contents of this book and without whom, its completion would not have been possible.

Ohio Veterans Plaza
Dedicated August 21-23, 1998

The Ohio Veterans Plaza is located adjacent to the east facade of the Senate Building at the Ohio Statehouse in downtown Columbus. It is a public recognition of the men and women from Ohio who served, and sometimes gave their lives, in the military service to our country. This expression honors their service in time of war or peace.

As restoration architect of the Capitol, Schooley Caldwell Associates was asked by the State of Ohio to work with a committee representing various veterans groups from around the State to create a dignified, permanent memorial with significant symbolic value. The design is "buildable" and practical to maintain. Funding for the Plaza was provided from the Statehouse Restoration project budget, the Capitol Square Review and Advisory Board, and the Capitol Square Renovation Foundation.

Design components of the Plaza includes two curved Ohio limestone walls, ten feet high and forty feet long, inscribed with actual correspondence sent home to family, friends and loved ones by soldiers.

Those correspondences are included in this publication. Additionally, we have included letters which were received by the committee but were not included on the walls.

Other features include small fountains, benches, plaques depicting the seals of the five branches of the armed services, inscribed names of all 88 Ohio counties with accompanying flag holders for ceremonial purposes, and a large, grassy lawn to commemorate the traditional parade ground atmosphere of the military encampment.

The Plaza also serves as a major entrance to the Capitol complex, used by all tour and school groups. The area features a drop-off space for buses and it is the primary means of access for people with disabilities. The entry steps (there are also ramped walkways) doubles as a podium for ceremonies, and there is provisions for portable sound systems as well as a connection to the Statehouse television production studio and communications system.

The Plaza and its design features not only commemorate the service of all veterans but serves as an appropriate educational vehicle for the many visitors and students who pass the Statehouse grounds every day.

Groundbreaking for the Plaza was held on September 18th, 1997 and dedication was held the weekend of August 21-23, 1998.

Letters Which Were Included As Part of The Ohio Veterans Plaza...

Dear Mom, Dad, and All,

It is foggy here most of the time and so we see very little sunshine. I even have to pray for myself once in a while. You get very jittery not knowing what may happen. You have only God to turn to for protection and guidance. Anything can happen and usually does. You die a thousand times and don't know it. Your mind wanders and you think of home, your folks, your girl. Will you ever see them again? Sure you will! "Nothing will happen to me," you say. "I'll watch my step." Yeah. You keep on walking, clinging to your rifle, finger itching on the trigger, waiting, waiting for something to move in the stinkin' jungle. Its dark as pitch. Its just a monkey or an elephant, or a jungle cat or a snake or one of your own men who got lost. Or maybe its the dirty, sneakin' enemy lying in wait, ready to make a bloody mess of you. You don't move.

Your Son,
George

Dearest Marge,

How does this letter find my little sis tonight? You were wondering what the name of my plane was. Its name (I should say her name) is "Shady Lady" and we have a large picture of a beautiful gal clothed scantily (but sufficiently) painted on the side of the nose by me. I'm going to get a picture taken of the crew beside it one of these days.

Sincerely Yours,
George (Killed In Action)

Dear Mom,

It seems so strange that I haven't heard anything from any of you since the middle of December, five months ago. We heard that food parcels can no longer be sent, to bad if true. It would be hard going if it weren't for the weekly Red Cross parcel. I know I'm a father by now but don't know whether I have a son or a daughter.

Your Son,
Laurence POW

Dear Marge,

You stated you had a good idea where I was or am. You haven't. I think I know where you think I am. I'm not! I could give you ten guesses and I'll bet you wouldn't come within a thousand miles of it. Anyway you needn't worry as I am in a much safer and better place than you thought I was. Perhaps soon I can tell you just where I am. Even after I tell you, you probably wont know where I'm located.

Love,
Joe

Dear Bill,

In just 21 days you will be 8 years old. Perhaps by the time you get this letter - if you ever do - and its extremely doubtful - you will be getting right alone towards 9 years. I wonder.

As I write this, I am in my "office" about 300 feet under the ground. Outside is the tunnel, which is hewn out of solid rock, I can hear the air rushing. I have just came back from a long trip all alone the front. I saw a few of my old friends. So many more are gone. They were brave men, fellow; the kind of guys I'd like you to be when you grow up. All of the troops have stood up in great style under the worst kind of punishment. We all, Americans and Filipinos alike, look to America for support. And we know that America won't let us down. Just as we haven't let her down. You see son, it means a lot to be an American. And I want you to be a good one. It will be a long, long time before I see you and your mother again. There is no more I can say. Be good, study hard, and don't forget me.

Happy Birthday Boy,
Dad POW - Killed In Action

Dear Mom,

We had a little tough luck last time. We took off to hit Tarawa. On our first bomb run, our bomb doors wouldn't open so we turned around to hit them again. We discovered we didn't have a full flight so, Boy! did all the Zeros flock to the kill. Twenty 20MM shells went into our ship plus uncountable 7.7 holes. All our engines were hit. Our controls were shot almost completely away. Our engineer wired up our rudder cable so we could fly the "Wake Island Sleeper." The elevator cable was so badly shot up he was afraid to try to fix it for fear it would snap the one remaining strand. Five of our crew were hlt.

When the old girl was kilt we started to lose altitude and it sure looked like our earthly days were over. We couldn't toss any guns overboard because the Zeroes, were really giving us hell. Our left inboard engine kept wind-milling along. We knew it had been hit bad. Finally, Warren sighted Nanumea. Andy told me to drop the wheels but our gear was shot up too bad. We decided to make a crash landing on a reef. It was during those hours that I realized what a fool I was to ignore a girl like Joan. I swore then that if God would spare us, I would ask her to marry me.

The right inboard engine had run for three hours without any oil. She was throwing red het metal and sparks. Any minute now we would catch on fire. Andy did one of the bravest things I've ever seen. He went back to his seat and took over again. The autopilot wouldn't hold it. I got the courage to Join him. The crew braced themselves. The ship started to ease down into the water. She began to grind and groan and screech as the coral cut out the ship's life. She finally stopped, like the queen she was. The old girl was through but she did a wonderful job.

Love,
Charles (Killed In Action)

Mr. Elmerick,

Thanks so much for your letter. I know right where post 221 is located and plan to pay the post a visit when I return. It makes us all here very proud to have the support of all the vets. We now share something with all of you. We also know it is up to us now to carry on and live up to the standards set by you and your fellow veterans. We will not let you down.

We've heard about the war protesters in the U.S.. The only thing that bothers me about it is that none of them realize that at least they're in a place where they can protest. That's more than the Kuwaiti people can say.

Thanks Again!
M.W.M.

Hi Folks,

   I suppose by this time the War Dept. has notified you about me. I am in a hospital in France it is a tent hospital. I was hurt quite badly and have lost my right leg, and also my little finger on my right hand, and my ring finger on my left hand. That is why the Red Cross is writing this for me. Please don't worry about me, for I am quite comfortable and getting good care, food and rest.

                    Your Son and Brother,
                    Vic

Dear Folks,

I stepped on a booby trap April 15. It sent a bullet through my left calf. It shattered the bone but I kept tellin the doc not to cut it off. He did a great job.

Yesterday a Captain and a SP/4 came in and presented me with the Purple Heart right in the ward. They pinned it on my pillow where everyone could see it. It brought a tear to my eye.

Take Care, Pray For Me.
Steve

Dear Darlene,

Yes, I've seen the Iraqi POWs. There just like normal people. Most were soldiers in their country by threat that if they didn't fight their families would be killed. Most surrendered. So when at first when we were returning them, they were killed. Its such a sad story. Then there are the babies that were in the wrong place at the wrong time. I can't wait to come home. Looks like May. Thank the Lord. I'm ready to get back to the great US of A.

Love,
Shirley

Dear Family,

Tell dad I have found the ideal thing for the farm. You have no doubt heard stories about the jeep. Well, that is not the half of it. I believe you could use them for anything. It is not true they will fly, but I have seen them do other things just as amazing. With one of them, we could make old Kate look sick. The jeep has a great future after this war. I am really sold on one.

Love,
Fred

My Dearest Joan,

Yesterday I was at a concentration camp. It so happened we captured a German supply train the night before. Four of us loaded up a truck with food and took it down there. I never want to see such a sight again. 14,000 starving, diseased, stinking people. It was terrible. Most of them were Jews Hitler had put away for safe keeping. Some of them had been in camps for 8 years. So help me, I cannot see how they stood it. No longer were most of them people but things that were once human beings.

As we pulled off the highway we had to shove them off the truck. They were dirty, walking skeletons, some to weak to walk. Some lay around dead where they had fallen. Others would fall as they tried to keep up with the truck. We stopped to unload the food and tried to keep them from crowding so we could unload but they were beyond reasoning. We had to start shoving them out of the road. They would just stand there, look right in your face and cry like a baby.

Finally, we took our guns and pointed them in their faces and they still stood there and bawled. We fired a few shots in the air and still we couldn't clear them. One woman could only cry and point at her mouth. Finally, we started to unload. We picked about 15 to help us. How those skinny fellows lifted those boxes is beyond me. Any number of them came up and touched us if they couldn't believe that we were actually there. One fellow had nothing to give of value, so he gave me his little yellow star. I'll send it to you.

That SS man I captured later in the day never came so near in his life to dying, I pointed my pistol right against his heart but I couldn't shoot him in cold blood.

Love,
Del

Dear Sharon,

     Ranger command sent me back to Pleiku. I was just there long enough for a clean uniform, a steak, a couple of beers and a nights sleep when I could close both eyes. Then they sent me to Ben Het.

     I am back with Bob. It looks like our fearless colonel has managed to banish both of his prize 8-balls to the farthest corner of the realm. Like all other camps, we're not allowed to fly the American flag. They say its because it is Vietnamese camp and we're just advisors. If I'm gonna fight over here, I'd like to fight under my own flag. I've run up the Ohio flag I found at Duc Co.

     What the hell, its got stars, its got stripes, its red, white and blue and it doesn't violate that idiot regulation. Besides its a bit of home.

              I Love You Pretty Lady,
                 Mark

Dear Ruth,

This is my first opportunity to write since I have been liberated. I am now in Camp Lucky Strike near Le Havre, France. I am in fine health. I find it difficult to write as I haven't heard from you since before my capture, and so I naturally don't know whether I am yours or just nobody's. I am very hopeful that you have waited, as you promised. Well, its time to eat again, so I will say, so long until next time. You will just have to sweat it out, like I am. Be Good

Just Like Always,
Milton

My Dearest, Darling Judy,

Writing to you on this day is the best way I know how to celebrate. Being with you at the close of war in Europe would be the highest and most glorious thing I could hope for. Today is VE day and everyone is celebrating but me. I will spend it in church and, darling, my glory-making will be held when I am once again back with the one I love -You. That will be my victory day. I am on the western coast of England. As I look out across the ocean, I strain my eyes trying to see the states.

Midnight, darling. I am staying with that family. I told you how swell they have been to me. The whole city is lit up. I overheard a little boy ask his mother, "mum what are all those lights?" She could not answer because her eyes were so full of tears. My thanks to you, my family, your family and especially to God.

Yours Always,
Ralph

My Darling,

After chow, we went back to the field and were told that we were to sleep there for the night. I laid me poncho in the very damp ground and put my sleeping bag on top of this and then spread the other half of the poncho over the bag. I wore my green pants, wool shirt, flannel dress shirt, field jacket, wool socks and my silver fox coat. Well, maybe it isn't silver fox but it is fur of some kind, probably field mice. I then climbed into the sleeping bag and zipped it up. The stars were really beautiful. I think I must have slept during the night because I dreamt of you. I probably would have frozen stiff if I hadn't.

All My Love Forever,
Tom

Darling,

Tonight is Christmas night. There is still no mail from you and I miss your letters very much. Letters have souls; they can speak; they have in them all the fires of our passions; they have all the tenderness, delicacy of speech and sometimes a boldness of expression beyond it.

All of my joys have nothing but the memory of the past. I still preserve the desire to be loved by you. My passion by right belongs to you, and you can in no way become disengaged. A love such as mine cannot be indifferent.

I recall your image in my mind. I incessantly seek for you. I shall still love you with all my soul till the last moment of my life. Goodnight, darling.

All my love,
Tommy

Dear Adrian,

Jerry can and does throw a lot of lead at night and whenever smoke blinds him. The SS troopers are true fanatics and there's no resting when they're around. It takes bayonets, guts and death to convince the Nazi that he'd better turn tail. The German matches you trick for trick and guts with guts. The man who said there are no atheists in foxholes had hit the nail on the head. When the sun goes down and darkness steals in, life to the infantryman becomes nothing more than a gust of wind. The nights are long, forgotten hours and cold and you are invariably dug in the middle of a big field, a grenade in one hand, more handy, and your other hand fingering your BAR - it's you and good old Mother Earth and God. To us, death is no distant unknown, God just a Sunday thought, and prayer a child's last daily must.

Albert, Jr.

Sallie Darling,

I can but realize the terrible ordeal you went through yesterday. I thanked God a thousand times one of those bombs did not hit the hospital. I was in the powder magazine in charge of an ammunition detail when the first bomb hit. My dear, you don't know how much I worried yesterday, not knowing if you were OK. I know you have to work without sleep and must be tired to death. I'm damned proud of you nurses. You are a real soldier and I'm trying to be one. I hear some planes roaring overhead but I think they're ours. Pray to God we get back home again. I love you.

Be careful, dear
Jerry

To the Reeses,

I was hoping to get glimpses of Saudi culture, but I've seen nothing yet except infinite expanses of desert. There is a constant wind blowing and the dust in the air makes visibility terrible. The wind blows little trails of sand across the dunes like spirits not at rest roaming the desert. It gives the illusion of a dream state. As a child, I learned about deserts. I'd never seen one except in movies and they don't even come within reach of the real thing. I feel like I've always been here. The place I sleep is my home. Ohio seems like a dream, intangible and far from my reach and I cling to it and memories of it because they are all I have. Memories can be trusted. The only other thing I trust is my M-16. I wonder how much I will change. I've seen what Nam did to men. I don't want to change. The hardest part of my life is coming.

Love to the family,
Brad

Dear Mom and Dad,

Sept. 22-44. Mission at Kassel, Germany. Went over target 2 times. Flak was plenty heavy, plenty holes in the planes. Some of the fellows had to land in Belgium because shot up too much (head navigator got us through the thick of the flak). Was off course. Then on again.

Sept. 22-44. Mission at Kassel, Germany. Went over railroad center. Plenty of flak, no fighters. I almost didn't get back today. My oxygen hose pulled loose and I passed out. The waist gunner saw me and got to me after about 5 min. God was with me. We fly again tomorrow. 5 1000 lbs. bombs.

Sept. 22-44. Mission at Kassel, Germany. Went over target so we had to go again to hit it today. We did. And I saw plenty. 2 planes went down over the targets, both by flak. One parachute come out of each, open up at 24000 feet. Plenty of flak. One of the fellows, a radio man I know, was killed on this raid. You never know when you get it around here. If God would only give us the power to make them quit right now so it won't go on any longer. Fly again tomorrow.

Sept. 22-44. Mission at Kassel, Germany. Went over target and we were on our own. Enemy fighters were in the area. I flew with another crew. Put me one raid ahead of my crew. We lost 20 bombers to enemy fighters and 7 from flak. Bad place Merseburg.

Jack
(Killed In Action)

My Dearest Joan,

As I was driving back from Suwon today, I saw a little girl about 5 or 6 lying in a ditch. She had a large cut on her leg that was still bleeding. The poor kid didn't have enough warm clothes, so I hopped out of the truck and put my battle jacket around her and stopped the bleeding. I took her to a house. Nobody knew she was hurt. Her parents were both killed.

It's not how many buildings get torn up - it's the kids that matter, hon. They haven't done anything to deserve what they're getting.

Always,
Steve

Dear Ettie,

A dream at last appears to be turning into reality. Tomorrow I am quite sure I shall be back in our homeland, the UNITED STATES OF AMERICA. It is with deep sense of emotion that I think of setting foot on our soil again, and I know that it is a privilege and a blessing. Many have gone from our shores never to return. On Monday, as darkness came, it began to get rough again. The ship tossed and bobbed on the ocean like a toy. When the waves hit the ship broadside they drove against our vessel with terrific force. A trip like this should convince anyone that there is a Supreme Master, a God who governs this and all other things in nature. Now the ship rides very smoothly, almost as if she knows she is nearing her berth. Now I am going to bed and dream of home. Perhaps in the morning the land will be there to greet us.

All my love,
Ed

Dear Bevie,

Today I went to a man's funeral I didn't even know. As his body passed by with a draped flag over his casket, I had a lump in my throat and a certain pride that only a man in the Army feels when his fellow American and fellow soldier gives his life so that fellowship can survive.

As I raised my rifle to fire the 21 gun salute, a tear ran down my cheek. When taps was playing, both eyes had tears in them. I looked into the faces. Their faces asking, why? Being a soldier, I know why. And the man I didn't know lying in the flag-draped casket, he knew also and died for it. You're asking yourself why? Because it's America. As I was looking at the faces, one was looking at me. He saw the tears in my eyes. He smiled gently and nodded as if to tell me how he felt. Somehow, the red, white and blue seems to draw people together in times of despair. No matter who or what they are. We know, Bevie, because the Major we laid to rest was black.

Love,
Your Richard

Dear Georgia,

Today was a tough one. It was crawling under real machine gun fire and the bullets were only 20 inches over our heads. If one was to get up on his knees or elbows, it would have been too bad. I admit I was a little nervous at first but once I was out there it wasn't so bad. We had to creep and crawl 100 yards. When I was through I was wringing wet with sweat. The dust was about an inch thick. I don't know what they'll think of next. But in all, it can't be as bad as today.

Your loving husband,
Nick

Dear Mom and Dad,

Well the day for which the world has been waiting for these many dreary years is now here with startling suddenness. This evening two air raid sirens began wailing long and loud to proclaim that Japan had accepted the surrender terms. Almost at once, soldiers began streaming from their barracks shouting, smiling, laughing, dancing and slapping each other on the back.

And yet, despite the atmosphere of joy and gaity, I could not help but notice the grim, unsmiling countenances of many overseas veterans. And I, too, felt rather sad. We could not help but think of the ones who will never know the joys of this day. These boys who sleep now in many foreign lands are the ones to whom the world should be eternally grateful. They too dreamed of their homes, their wives and sweethearts and longed for the day they could go back. I, for one, will never forget them. In my heart I will always see those rows and rows of little white crosses I saw so many times in Africa and Italy. It's up to you and me and the rest of us to remember how much was given. Personally, I feel rather humble.

Your son,
Ralph

Greetings, Bellefontaine:

Personal thoughts aside, the bottom line is that the President ordered us here. I took an oath. It's my job to obey orders and get the mission accomplished. After all, it's what you - the public - pay me for. We are very fortunate to receive your local support like that of the majority of average Americans. I can remember growing up in the 60s and 70s, supporting the war effort with a sense of pride for our troops in Southeast Asia. It wasn't the popular thing to do back then, but at our house, we were taught a sense of respect for country. As long as one U.S. fighting man or woman was there in harm's way, we felt it our civic duty to respect and support them. I was truly embarrassed for the way a vast majority of my "fellow countrymen/women" behaved during those turbulent years.

P.A.

To My Journal:

The terrain here is beautiful. The ocean is right close, spacious rice paddies, towering mountain ranges and green jungle. The sunsets and sunrises are a work of art by God's hand. Even though the enemy is near, there is a very peaceful feeling here. Yesterday on recon we walked through part of a hamlet I'd not been in before. It was like Alice's Wonderland: Villagers in rice paddies planting shoots, irrigating, some cutting and bundling new rice shoots to be transported to the watery paddies. A section of paddy was set aside to grow purple orchids that were beautiful. In the trees, the trails were like walking through a fantasy forest.

D.A.G.

My Darling Blue Eyes,

Here's your old man again. I hope everything is OK with you and our little champ. I'll bet the little rascal really keeps you busy. I enjoyed the V-Mail Valentine. It's things like that, that makes a guy love and adore a sweetheart like you. Oh, it's impossible to express my feelings on paper. I would take you in my arms, look into your blue eyes and tell you everything so easy. No one could ever come so close to me. You're the blood in my veins, the food I eat, the one I dream of, oh, just life itself built around you. You make me tingle all over and feel like I am sleeping on blue clouds of love.

Love,
Daddy

Dear Adnelle,

It is a quiet evening in France. As night settles over our camp, the drowsy mooing of cattle and other familiar farmyard sounds mingle with the occasional distant boom of artillery - a strange contrast. The farming countryside is very pretty. The trees are if anything more luxurious than in England and flowers plentiful. This evening I talked for quite a while with some French people who live nearby and had a lot of fun. ILs sont blanchet mon chemise et mon culottes. Comprenez vous? They seemed to enjoy hearing the words from us too. The people are very friendly and the children (les enfants) especially are frequent visitors.

Darling, I am trying to imagine in this beautiful countryside you and I are watching the fading sunset together. It is a pleasant thought, dearest, and one which I am determined to fulfill.

Avec tout mon amour,
Virgil

Dear Eileen,

I was appointed squad leader position today, which means my hard work is being noticed. Everything I learn here will help me later in life. 1. Never assume anything. 2. No matter how bad you don't want to do something, see it through and make the best of it. 3. Home is where you make it. 4. Make things happen for yourself. Take charge of your life. 5. Don't take little things in life for granted. 6. If you really love someone, they're always with you no matter where you are. 7. Teamwork. 8. Friends are invaluable. 9. Trust in yourself and your first instinct. 10. Don't lose touch with your Creator.

Love,
Dave (Killed In Action)

Hi Everybody,

I'm a company runner now, a good job because it's a lot safer. I wish you all wouldn't worry so much about me. Sometimes we're just on the move and they cannot mail our letters.

We have been in combat 16 straight days. Slowly we are reaching the 38th parallel again. We are fighting the Chinese now and they are harder to fight. They are smart people. They have tunnels going through all these mountains. Hill 930 was about 3000 feet, but 930 means 930 meters. Every hill we have to attack is named by height. Some of our objectives before 930 was 260, 303, 390, 430, 720, 869, down again to 315, up to 930. Hill 303 we had a lot of trouble on. It took 2 ½ days & nights to take it. But we foxed them. We set fire to the whole mountain & boy did they run. We got about 95 prisoners. Say hello to everyone.

Your loving son,
Walter (Killed In Action)

Dear Folks,

My first time on night guard. I saw men moving up on us. I saw one man pointing a gun at me. Then it came, artillery in close, coming closer. The man pointing the gun never went down. I found out the next day it was a fence post with a board nailed on. That was the night I learned how to tell by the sound of a shell how and where it will land. With artillery shells you have plenty of time to take cover. Mortar is heard a split sec. before it hits. Many a man was killed by mortar for that reason. But during an attack, both mortar and artillery is falling. All you can do is ask God for guidance and keep moving ahead. That way, most falls to your rear. In battle, a man is an ostrich, I once hid behind a little bush and felt as safe as I do now. A bush means as much to an 88 as a grape being crushed between your fingers.

Love,
Bud

DEAR PARENTS:

DEEPLY REGRET TO INFORM
YOU THAT YOUR SON WAS KILLED
IN ACTION 19 FEBRUARY 1945 AT IWO
JIMA VOLCANO ISLANDS IN THE
PERFORMANCE OF HIS DUTY AND
SERVICE OF HIS COUNTRY. WHEN
INFORMATION IS RECEIVED
REGARDING BURIAL YOU WILL BE
NOTIFIED. TO PREVENT POSSIBLE
AID TO OUR ENEMIES DO NOT
DIVULGE THE NAME OF HIS SHIP OR
STATION. PLEASE ACCEPT MY
HEARTFELT SYMPATHY. LETTER
FOLLOWS.

A.A.V. LIEUT GENERAL USMC

My Dear Mrs. Davis,

I have been trying to send you a few lines since Iwo Jima but due to censorship and a rule which keeps us from writing to casualties' families, it was impossible. One of the Marines from our outfit is going to the States, and he is going to mail this. It's not the right thing to do but in my own heart, I do not think it wrong. As you probably know, Jerry was my best pal. We had been in all the invasions side by side. We got wounded rather closely together and shared our hospital days. We have shared foxholes, clothing, money, packages from home - we were that close. Although I have never had the pleasure of meeting you, I feel that I really know you. You see, Jerry and I shared our letters from our mothers because the letters were so alike. I don't think I can ever obtain a pal who can fill Jerry's shoes. He was not only a "regular fellow" but also a darn good Marine - the best. He had a lot of courage and guts. Not only have you lost a son, I my best pal and the Marine Corps one of the best Marines, but the world has lost one of its greatest men. I feel proud to have known him and to have him like me the way he did.

Yours truly,
George

I see the visions of green trees blowing
gently in a
cool summer breeze.
There's a yellow tint over everything
like somehow, this
vision is from my past.
Children are playing in the street and
cars drive by on
the freeway.
I'm standing in the yard with my friends
all around me
talking,
but I'm looking away as if turning my
attention toward
the surroundings.
My life passes before my eyes, all the
childhood memories
I'm in my own little world, but my world is
these very
people and objects that surround me.
I suddenly realize where I am, how important
this place is.
I gain unending respect for this place
and these people.
In my mind's eye, nothing is as beautiful as
Ohio in the
summer,

and nothing is so precious as that little group
around me,
       my friends and family.
My life passes before my eyes, all the
childhood memories
       come back,
everything that influenced me and made me
who I am.
       I'd never realized how special and
       important it is, my
home, my people, my memories.
       Wouldn't it be a tragedy?
Wouldn't it be unfair?
       Would these people forget?
Would life go on as usual?
       Would my message have an effect?
Would my spirit live on in my friends?
       Would they carry on and still keep the
       faith?

A Marine

A Memory:

Here in Italy, wino is ten cents a quart and since it's pure we find it's a nice substitute for vasser. I hear some Canadian soldiers using a few curse words I have never heard before, complaining about the cold rain and mud of Corsica. I see skinny cows pulling crude wooden plows over rich black earth. I look skyward and I can see houses hanging from the mountain like picture slides. When I enter a town, a flock of unwashed children pull at my coat and beg for gum. Then it's off to midnight mass. A prayer to the Virgin Mary. "Hail Mary full of grace. Please let me stay alive so I can go home all in one piece. It's a blend of smoky yellow candles, floating garlic aroma and a few "dominus sa vestal." I watch pilots playing poker with the sky as the limit. Money is of little importance when you realize that when tomorrow dawns there is the possibility you will not be around to spend it.

Joe

Dearly Beloved,

He was a short, fair lad and fair-haired,
somehow suggesting your brother Lou. He
was soft spoken, quiet and liked to play bridge.
I got to know him on the ship. He asked to be
transferred to submarine duty. Many a night
we would stand by the rail, the star studded
sky overhead, the swish of the wondrous
Pacific accompanying our talk, only the
phosphorescent gleam of minute life lighting
up the darkness below and we would talk. He
would talk, mainly, and I would listen. He told
me how much he loved his girl. We discussed
the advisability of marriage during these
perilous times and I could see he craved
encouragement from me, and I gave it
wholeheartedly, for I feel that even a token of
love snatched from the jaws of danger is
worthwhile, if it is with the one beloved, and
then there is always Hope and Faith. And there
are always beautiful memories to relive and to
dream and re-dream and to comfort one; and
above all to light up the vision of the time to
come. I did not see him again after we landed.

The next day was the Banzai attack - that furious, raging, mad onslaught made without apparent rhyme or reason, in a frenzy of despair and desire for self-immolation. They came and told me he had been killed - it is best you not look at him. And so I can best see him as I saw him last, whole, alive, dreaming dreams and speaking of Love. He was too young to have known his life for long - too young to be knowing Death for so long.

I love you my angel,
Morry

Dear Sis,

*She says how after they bomb us flat, we'll
need hundreds of bulldozers to scrape it off. Then
she tells us of strikes (at home), etc., and our wives
going out with other men while we waste our time
over here. "Why don't you go home ?" she asks. It's
pretty good and we sure get a lot of laughs out of it.
She calls herself "Tokyo Rose - Our Friendly
Enemy." I don't tell Mom this ' cause you know
Mom - she'll worry herself sick. The water situation
is still pretty bad. We still wash and bathe in the
ocean which is pretty salty. I think it will get better
later on. I still have your picture and the fellows
think it's swell too.*

> *All my love*
> *From your little brother,*
> *Billy Joe*

Dearest Mom and Dad,

I met this S/Sgt. Barry the first day I was in the ward in the "Krankenhaus." Usually the discussions start with combat experiences, but soon our discussion swung from the war to home and the folks back home. Before long I had all my pictures out of my wallet. He was with the 82nd Airborne Div. ever since their first combat jump in North Africa. In all, he jumped all five missions - N.A., Anzio and Salerno, Normandy on D-Day and, finally, Belgium. He was hit in Belgium. He showed me a picture of himself as a civilian and his hair was very dark. Now his hair is snow white and there were also lines of worry on his face.

Oceans of love,
Fritz

Dear Folks,

Last night on the radio we heard a lot of Christmas carols. Even the German radio stations were playing Silent Night. One of the fellows hung up his stocking to sort of carry out the old tradition, you know. This morning one of the guys had filled it up with a lot of hard candy. So you see, there is a Santy Claus after all.

Love,
Bob

My Dearest Wife and Son,

I have seen one of the worst atrocities
than I thought humanly possible. Last Friday,
there were 1100 Russian and French prisoners,
possibly one American, in a little town. The
Germans knew we were coming and they had
to move quick. They had these men dig two
huge deep graves for themselves. But we came
too fast for them and they had to act quicker so
they crammed these men into a little brick barn
and spread straw all around and saturated it
with gasoline. Honest honey, it was the
awfulest sight I have ever seen. One day while
I was up with the company I did something
that has been bothering me ever since, even to
the point of dreaming about it and it has really
haunted me. Now, since seeing this, I don't feel
as bad about it at all.

All My Love Forever,
Paul

Dear Mom & Family,

We had a big snow storm this afternoon. I was talking to an English fellow the other day. He said since the Yanks came to this country, the living has changed, the women have changed and now he thinks the weather is changing. He said this was more snow than he had seen in a long time. I told him that he ought to see some of the ones we have at home.

Love,
Earl

Mom and Dad,

Well, I know why I'm fighting. It's the same thing Dad did in 1917 & 1918, so we wouldn't have to fight, but we are. I'm fighting so my kids, or the rest of the fellows like me's kids won't have to do it. I want to have a family. I want Louise as my wife. She's the one I love, Mom, and always will. You knew that a long time ago. In case I never see her again, please tell her that I really have loved her and we would have been happy together, that I'll be waiting for her always. Also tell her to find a swell fellow who can love her ½ as much as I did and live happy with him.

I remain loving you always, forever,
Jack (Killed In Action)

To My Journal:

June 30 - While we were sweeping, air strikes were called on the Hill. At 5:30 PM we found a trail leading up. The word was passed to "fix bayonets" at that point. Everybody thought it was a joke. Then a man in front of me tripped a booby trap grenade and received a sucking chest wound. The 1st platoon was pinned down by sniper fire from a bunker on top of the forward ridge line. After three hours of fighting, we took the hill. But 1st platoon took eight dead, seventeen wounded 2nd platoon, seven dead, sixteen wounded. During the fight, Lima company came up the hill behind the enemy position.

July 4 - Today we are spending Independence Day on top of Hill 728. The skipper is trying to arrange some kind of celebration. On the resupply run today, the helicopter brought cokes, C rations, letter mail. Sometimes we get fresh fruit, juices, smokes, candy, etc. From this hill, you can see the Laotian border off over mountain ranges and rolling hills. We are not trying to make contact with the enemy because we have no blocking force. We are reconnaising.

D.A.G.

Dear Mother and Dad,

I'll start by saying that my points are now 54 - I got 5 for one more battle star which the division now wears and 5 more for the Bronze Star. I got it for a patrol into enemy lines one night when we were in the Bulge. I remember the exact time because three of us spent two hours on our stomachs not over 15 feet from a German machine gun nest - it was cold as hell and I was sweating like it was June.

Right now we are occupying a zone and trying to get things straightened out between the Russians, Czechs, Partisans and the peace-loving American army. We have the Russians near us. They are quite an outfit. Not particularly well dressed soldiers but they are plenty tough and darn hard to get along with. They reflect the attitude of Stalin in all actions. And they trust us about as far as I can throw a horse. But by being diplomatic, we get along and I hope we'll do the same in the future.

All my love,
Phil

Hi Grandma,

Here I am alive and the war is over. I am writing you from Japan in Tokyo Bay where everything is quiet and that seems funny doesn't it? We were among the first ships in. You have probably heard of Japan's volcanic Fujiyama mountain. Well I saw it real close. I watched it at sunset and it was the most beautiful scene I have ever witnessed. This is a rich and beautiful land. Well your prayers were answered and I came through a lot of tough spots and am very happy and thankful. I am really anxious to get out and get home and stay there and live like a human. An awful lot of our boys won't be coming back.

I remain your grandson,
Clyde

Dear Jackleen,

This is destined to be a sad letter because that is how I'm feeling. I promise this will be the only sad letter you receive. I know we promised faithfully never to write a letter like this. Indulge me this once. Do you realize how much those last several days together meant to me? Then you know how much the last seven years have meant. How lonely my life would have been had it not been for you. When I think back, I feel that we must have lived two lifetimes worth - and I would gladly live two more. The prospect of spending a year separated from you leaves me numb. I am consoled by the thought that you are living as normal an existence as possible. I pray that you are. I have spent all these lines telling you how sad I am and now I say you shouldn't be. These thoughts will not be repeated. I will learn to live with them tucked away. Occasionally I will call one forth, savor it for awhile and tuck it away again. Did you see me as I waved goodbye to your airplane? I was standing on the car but you probably were on the other side of the plane.

All my love,
King Edward IV
(Killed In Action)

A Memory:

We parachuted into Normandy six hours before D-Day. I was all alone in the dark except for three live cows and five bloated dead cows. I sat on a rock and was spellbound by the beautiful fireworks that lit up the sky. I felt relaxed and was thinking, "this is a nice, quiet, peaceful war." However, when I saw fiery sparks curving towards American planes the fireworks lost most of their beauty.

J.F.

To The Editor,

As I read the Christmas note which came from Akron, an exhilaration exploded within me. It was nothing easily perceived but it was something which immediately attracted me. It was a feeling of collective consciousness. Most likely it's an energy which has always been there - somewhere within me. And now I'm aware that feeling is not only within me, but it is also with me. Thank you - and Merry Christmas!

M.P.S.

Dear Mother,

I know that we in the Army are called upon to sacrifice more than the people in civilian life. I know you're going through everything I am, except the physical end of it. And being a mother I'm sure you would do that if you could. When these people came up to us and were just satisfied to look at us, well, I sure did feel pretty damn small. And I couldn't even say a word, in spite of the fact I don't like the feeling of being gazed at like a rare specimen in a lab of some sort. Now if I should feel like this, I'm wondering just what the people back there who let us down should feel like. Yes, I want you to show this letter to those people back there who cried like babies when they had their drinks cut off at twelve o'clock, and I want you to show it to the people who think this war should have been over some time ago, and to any other person who thinks Elmer Davis is just trying to sell war bonds. I really can't put into words the feeling that came over me when I saw those people. Nordhausen was just small fry compared to some of those places. Freedom is a wonderful thing when you take what they took for three years. Every one of them was sure the Americans would come.

Your loving son,
Jim

Hi Folks,

It's the day after Christmas here in sunny Saudi. Our Christmas was not the best I've ever had, but not too bad. Christmas eve, some of the mechanics came around singing carols. It was unexpected and did a lot to raise spirits! My tent mates and I decorated the little tree you sent, made some of that Wassail stuff (not bad!) and opened presents. It was a nice, peaceful evening. The pot-bellied stove and the Christmas candles set a homey atmosphere. Yesterday, Christmas day, we had Christmas dinner. The mess hall outdid themselves! We even got the Saudi version of a White Christmas - a huge sand storm! We told ourselves it was Saudi snow!

Love you,
Chip

Dear Dad,

Three days ago, our company was mortared and received grenades and scattered small arms fire. The third platoon leader was killed, the first platoon leader wounded and eighteen others were evacuated. I didn't get a scratch, but I have never been so scared in all my life. Dad, I saw the sunrise that morning and, along with others, sat for hours in disbelief. I must have thanked the Lord a hundred times since for that sunrise. We headed back. I saw my point man go down. When I got to him he was unconscious, shot through the chest and back. I slapped his face and told him to wake up, this was no time to be sleepin' on the job. He came to, in pain but OK. My RTO did a fine job calling in support. After going through that and seeing how all of these "scared" men become strong, good fighters, you know I can't help but respect their courage. I can't help but love them.

Keep in touch,
Bud

Hi Folks,

We'll be going to the port in a couple of days to pick up our brand new M1A1 Abrams tanks. I saw them earlier this week, super nice, straight out of Lima. Go ahead, Baghdad, make my day! Maybe we've finally outlived the Vietnam stigma. I pray it doesn't wither away when the casualties start. The soldiers over here are among the finest, best trained men and women who've ever served the nation. They are meeting the challenge with exceptional skill, courage and dedication. I am proud to be with them. As the deadline approaches, please don't worry. It's surprising but I feel pretty calm. I've prepared and trained my people as best I can. I've made my peace with the Lord. What ever happens, He will mean it to be. Been listening to the radio and none of it is very encouraging. It's hard to believe Saddam really thinks he can best us! Is he nuts? It's nine PM. Three hours til the deadline.

Love to all,
Chip

Dear Son,

Just across the channel from me is Bataan. I've been there. Our men were brave men. Here we have gathered once again to hold. And we shall. In the meantime, fellow, remember to say your prayers for all of us - the ones who'll never see their sons again - and the ones of us who still hope to. Take care of mother. Be the man I know you are. Be a real soldier of Bataan. Know how much I love you - want to be with you - I treasure the two little snapshots I was able to save of you and mother. I'm a major now, son. I hope I've made you proud.

Love you boy,
Dad POW /
Killed In Action

Dear Dawn,

It is hard for me to tell a little girl how much I love her, but someday you will know that it is very much. Did you know that from our house to Vietnam is more than 6000 miles? The next letter you get will be from Vietnam. Be sure and say your prayers before you go to bed and I will remember to say mine. When we get to Vietnam, I will be very busy. When you are busy, time passes very quickly.

Love,
Daddy (Killed In Action)

Hi Hon,

   This morning I had my first combat assault. Took off at 0710 with five gun ships. We had to take three lifts into the LZ. No friendlies on the ground so we really covered the LZ as the slicks came in! None of the slicks took a hit in my LZ! If it had been real hot we probably couldn't have suppressed all the ground fire. The best part of the day was we brought everyone back, although five ships got hit in various places. Anyway, I did real well and learned a lot and that's the important thing.

   Lovies,
   Me (Killed In Action)

Dear Dad,

   I thought I'd write you because I want to tell you some things I don't want Mom to hear. We can hear the bombs and artillery. I get worried at times but then I stop and think of everything you and the Corps taught me. You surprise yourself how far back you can go and remember things you have been taught. And I had one hell of a teacher (you).

   I love ya, Dad
   Ponch

Dear Ernestine,

     Many of us gathered around the radio at the Service Club to hear the President's prayer for the invasion. Darling, this date the whole world has been waiting for; and we know it brought sorrow to many a person - sister, brother, mother and father, friends, relatives. There are men shedding blood for our freedom. How fortunate we are here in the States. Let us not be unmindful that over there men are giving their lives in order that we may have freedom of religion, speech, fear, and want.

               Love,
               Wayne

Dear Folks,

I was just noticing a guy filling his ammo belt with cigarettes. I once saw a cartoon by Mauldin of two guys in a fire fight & when trying to get ammo out of their belt they both had all cigarettes. I saw that exact situation actually happen once. We were getting so we're hurting for ammo.

Love,
Lindy

My Darling Melinda,

I played those letters like a pianist would play the notes of a thrilling sonata: My darling Melinda! Has it ever occurred to you that I have never heard anyone speak your name? That is only one of a million things I have never experienced about you. The softness of your arms stealing around my neck. Your impatient kicks when I held you and you did not want to be held. Have I ever seen your sleep-filled eyes, or the yawns that say, "I want to go to bed." I often wonder what you think about. No doubt, very wonderful things, but it shall remain an unfathomable mystery. To us, and to you, the mind of your babyhood shall be unwritten history. The cost of this war will never be measured in dollars and cents, and who can weigh the cost of the longings of one million men? Goodnight, Melinda. May your dreams be sweet.

Daddy

Hi Mom & Dad,

I got a drill sergeant who is not human, I don't think. It's going to be real tough for the next 7 weeks. There's no heat in here either. You only get 5 minutes to eat your food and I was able to finish half my lunch today. My tendons are hurting still. I don't know how long I'll be able to last with them like this but I'm going to try and see. I don't know when I'll be allowed to make phone calls. Would like to hear from you.

Love,
Doug

Lori,

Well, by now you know what's going on over here. Yes, I'm a little scared. Sometimes I don't know if I can handle squad leader. I have 6 other guys working for me and they all look to me for answers. Sometimes I wish I was a private. We watch the planes go over and can hear the bombs when they hit. Just waiting for the time to push North. I don't know what to write but I don't want to stop. I feel closer to everybody when I write. Sorry this letter is sloppy. I'm writing by flashlight.

> *Love ya,*
> *Rich*

Dear Mom, Dad, Karen, Friends,

In the very near future the undersigned will once more be in your midst, dehydrated and demoralized, to take his place again as a human being with the well known forms of freedom and justice for all, to engage in life, liberty and the somewhat delayed pursuit of happiness. He might be a little Asiatic from Vietnamese-itis and overseas-itis and should be handled with extreme care. A little time in the land of the Big PX will cure this problem. Show no alarm when he insists on carrying a weapon at all times or looks around for his steel pot when offered a chair. Keep cool when he pours gravy on his dessert or mixes peaches with his Seagrams. Be tolerant when he takes his blanket and sheets off is bed and puts them on the floor to sleep. Abstain from saying things like Nook Maum, rice, fish, powdered eggs, dehydrated potatoes, filled milk. Do not get upset when he washes his plate with the toilet brush. Be especially watchful when he is in the presence of a girl. Keep in mind that under that tanned, rugged mean looking exterior, there is a heart of gold. By no means

plan his leave for him. Fill the ice box with
beer, get out the civvies, fill the car with gas
and get the women and children off the streets,

BECAUSE THE KID IS COMING HOME!

Daryl J.

Dear Mildred,

Today was a big day for me, and I had a ring side seat at one of the world's most historic events, the official surrender of the Japanese. We dropped our hook outside the breakwater. All around us were innumerable combat ships. Around them swarmed landing craft of all descriptions, hurrying their human cargo ashore that they might have a large show of force on hand. Overhead hundreds of B-29 bombers droned their way, then fighter planes in even larger numbers. If the Japanese signatories of the peace which was being signed on the USS Missouri only a stone's throw from us had any doubt left, they had only to scan the water around them and gaze into the sky. It was truly a magnificent show.

Love,
John

Hello Chris,

Prayers were answered when the chemicals used became ineffective as the wind changed and they blew back on Iraqi troops. How astounding! I am here to give glory to God. I became very disheartened during all of this and wondered would I ever see America again. How are we going to get me? Perhaps on the wings of angels.

Love,
Gail

Dear Mom & Dad,

     Hi! I'm in Saudi Arabia. The mission that lies ahead of this division is awesome. It is one that brings great pride to me and makes the hair stand up on the back of my neck thinking about the honorable profession I am in. Regardless of my personal convictions, I will follow the decisions made by the leaders of our great country because I trust in them that they are to make the decisions that will keep our country great and I will, if called upon, give my life for that. Trust in the Lord and pray for the brave men & women here. I feel comfortable with my life & soul right now. Please do not open the enclosed letter. If the time comes that you need to open it (you know when that will be), please do it in the presence of Janice. I pray that I will be able to destroy it a few months from now. Tell everyone hi! and I'll see you the fourth of July.

              Love & prayers,
              Rod

Dear Folks,

I saw a woman in the Philippines pounding meal from grain, likely rice, with a large weight hung by a pole and counterbalance arrangement, and a large bowl. It reminded me of the pictures in our history books of the colonies. That's why I think there is a lot of opportunity left in the world for expansion of industry. If we could show the people how to produce more with the same labor, it would create more demand for our products and promote a healthy trade. Their standard of living would go up and the world would demand some of the things we have, too. With a little education, these people could adapt themselves to a higher scale of living, making for a better world all around.

Your son,
Judge

Dear Folks,

Well I guess this will be my Christmas letter to all of you for the year 1970. All who always get together to celebrate Christ's birthday. Right now I am sitting on a jungle-covered hilltop - a setting sun. It is very hard to get in any sort of Christmas spirit as every day is the same - tromp through the jungle and hunt poor Charlie. We will be on our firebase for Christmas, but no matter where we are, everyone's thoughts will be of home. In a way, I am thankful of being away from home over the holidays. It makes you realize just how important family relationships really are. Vietnam has taught me another thing also and that is the value of life. It is my firm belief that God loves Charlie Cong just as much as he loves us. In war, he is on everyone's side. It is just because the family of man is so ignorant and selfish and refuses to practice the love that all religions teach that we have war today. The other day, we killed a Montagnard. He was called an enemy as he indeed had a Soviet rifle and was working for the VC harvesting their rice. No doubt he would have fired at us had he seen us first. But as I stood looking down at his bullet-riddled body, covered only by a loin cloth, I felt only sorrow. He was not my enemy. The VC indoctrinated him, handed him a rifle and sent him on his way. No, this "enemy" just like all other war casualties, is a victim. Man's failure to accept Christ's message, Peace on Earth, Goodwill Toward Men: the day after Christmas, we all go back to our selfish ways. Diplomacy has failed to bring peace. I guess religion is our only hope - that and every man's willingness to swallow a little pride and replace it with understanding and love.

Love,
Curt

DEAR SUZIE,

THIS IS IT BABY IM COMING HOME!!!

Jim

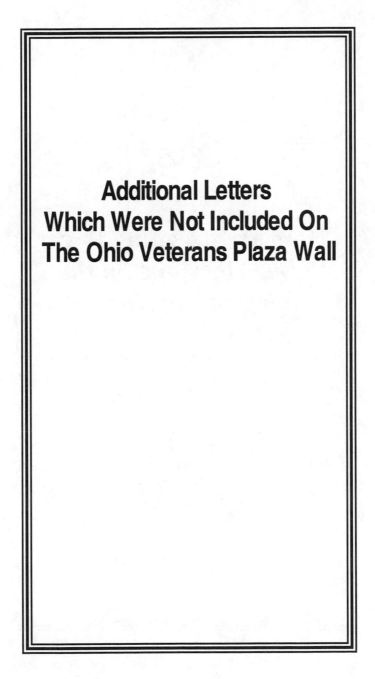

**Additional Letters
Which Were Not Included On
The Ohio Veterans Plaza Wall**

Theme...
DOMESTIC

"How are we going to get home? Perhaps on the wings of an Angel"

World War II

Dear Mother,

   We moved again. This time it's in a room with 40 of us, but they promise to partition off little rooms for us. After the lights manage to go out every evening at dusk, from then on it's candles.
   We are washing out of our helmets. My hair hasn't been washed for 3 weeks so I think I had better break down and use the dry shampoo I have. Sure have plenty of it and haven't even tried it yet. My hands are so cold writing this I can hardly hold the pen, but C'est la guerre.

Love,
Ethel

Korea

Hi Everybody,

We have been on the move pretty much. I'm up to Corporal. So when I come back, I'll have two stripes on my arm with a long red stripe in my blue trousers. It's just tradition in the Marine Corps. I look like an old man. I got a beard about two inches long and I've got that shining bracelet on my arm. The cigarettes didn't last long. Buddies you know and more buddies. Ha. Ha.

Thanks for everything.

> *Your loving son,*
> *Walter (Killed In Action)*

World War II

Dear Daughter,

I am proud and happy that you remembered me on Father's Day. Your greeting card is propped against your picture on my dresser. Your Daddy has gone away across the water for a while, but he hasn't forgotten you. He only wishes he could sweep you off your feet so you could hug him real tight. He would like to hear you say, "Hi Da-a-dee" once again. And Marcia, in his leisure time, your Daddy is exploring the shore of the largest ocean in the world and he is finding a lot of seashells which he is going to string into a necklace for you. He only wishes you were here to help him pick them out.

Love,
Daddy

World War II

Dear Mother,

Today is your birthday and my thoughts have been with you all day. I often think how fortunate we were not to know what would follow in the years after I last left you. Little did we realize that I would be writing you from a foreign land on your next three anniversaries and each time from a different country. I hope this may be the last. What other boy has such a swell mother as I? As I look back across the years, I see that we kids owe so much to you. Your faith in the Almighty, your honesty and integrity to your ideals and your bright outlook on life have inspired us all. Most of all, though, I believe I like you willingness to take up for the underdog. You have made sacrifices for us that we can never repay; the most we can do, it seems, is pay the interest on this big debt in love and devotion. I'll be very honest I don't know how old you are. Of course, I realize that many years ago, you passed the date the women quit telling their birth dates.

I hope both you and Dad are feeling well this spring.

Goodnight, Mom
Fred

World War II

Dear Son,

From far across the water on a strange land, your Daddy is sending a wish to you, my son. Your mother can read this to you. From within my heart I pray that this war of which your Dad is a part is not being fought in vain. I pray that you, my son, never have to take up arms against an enemy. I pray that your days of childhood and schooling are heaped full of joys and few sorrows. I pray that you will grow up into a fine young man and someday take a wife as lovely and grand as your mother; that you may have a home with children as fine as you yourself. May the good Lord above watch over you and you, in your manly way, watch over your mother until my return.

Kenneth

Korea

Kids,

I'm going overseas and will be gone for a long time. Both of you will have grown up. I hope we won't have to difficult a time getting to know each other again. Daddy would like to take you and Mommy with him but war might break out and I surely don't want to subject you to the hells of war and all the hardships that accompany it. Daddy would rather be separated from you and is willing to give up his life for you and Mommy rather than have you suffer a single hardship.

> *All my love forever,*
> *Daddy*

Vietnam

Hello,

Dad, don't think I don't enjoy reading your letters. I guess we never really did communicate but always talked at each other. Your letters give me a chance to see you and appreciate your ideas.

Love,
Jim

World War II

Dear Mother and Dad,

Today is Easter Sunday, an Easter unlike any other which I have spent before and which God willing, we shall never spend again. Our church is somewhat different than the one at home. For the roof we had the sky above and for light and heat we had the sun beating down with all its might. For seats we had modern boxes on old Mother Earth. Palm and coconut trees overhead did their best to provide shade, but usually gave it up as a bad job and instead threw coconuts at us at the most inopportune moments. In the background, planes were taking off and landing, warming up with a mighty roar that at times blotted out the words of the chaplain as much as cars screeching to a stop outside the church at home. Overhead, our planes drone on, giving us protective covering, for which we are thankful.

Your loving son,
Wayne

World War II

Dear Dad,

Since I have always been writing my letters to Mom, I will write this one especially to you.

Please don't try and work before you are able. I have had a lot of time to think since I have been in the army and I have decided where I belong. After seeing these people over here farm it sorta gives me yearning to show them a few things. One fellow had two ox`s and two mules pulling a little old forked stick (which they call a plow) and I believe old Snip could have pulled two of them.

Your son,
Johnny (Killed In Action)

World War II

Dear Mom and Dad,

I've been to church 19 times since I've been here. I have 11 more to go to finish up the Novena so you keep praying for me as you have been so far and if God watches over me as he has in the past, I'll see you soon at home. Could you stand that? Ha. Ha. I know you and Dad miss me as much as I miss you. Someday it will all be over. A lot of Moms and Dads won't see their son again. Just in case I do get mine in my last few raids, you and Dad take it like you should. That's all a fellow thinks about, will I see them again. So don't worry, God has a day for all of us.

I miss and love you both,
Your son, Jack (Killed In Action)

Theme...
SERVICE LIFE

"I got a drill sergeant who is not human, I don't think."

World War II

Hello Sweetheart,

The long looked for day is at long last at hand. Victory in Europe is ours. It's a very strange day, even we had expected it to be so very much different, and I imagine the folks at home picture the boys here going wild with joy, but they don't seem to think there is too much to rejoice about. They certainly aren't richer materially nor in friendships and all they seem to want to do is lay in the grass under the sun and enjoy the grand feeling of complete safety and security.

As I write this, we are somewhere in Austria near great, snow covered peaks rising in the distance. They certainly looked forbidding when they first came into sight. We thought we would have to pursue the Germans through them. Prisoners by the thousands are going past. Our absolute indifference to them means we haven't even guards on them. This is a very quiet, solemn day.

All my love,
Eddie

World War II

My Dearest Sis, Billy & Jimmy:

I guess you know Patton was a little slow crossing the Rhine. Ask Louise which regiment of which division was the first infantry regiment across the Rhine. Did I ever tell you I was at President Truman's house? A buddy of mine was trying to get into West Point and lived in the same town as Truman. In fact, he went with his daughter. He and I went on a pass one weekend to Wash. & he thought of Sen. Truman & daughter. He finally got hold of "Harry's" residence and talked to Mary Margaret. She invited us up. Harry gave us a cigar & Mrs. Truman served us Coca-Cola and sandwiches. Then Margaret took us to the zoo in the family car. We had a swell time. I was just wondering if Harry couldn't get me out of the army some way.

Love,
Bill

Peacetime

Dear Mom,

Last Sat. the five boys in our room went to Mount Fujiyama and climbed to the top of it. We drove up as far as we could in the weapons carrier about 7500 feet and slept. Then we started up on foot with canteens of water and three K rations. We started hollering and we got an answer from some girls and boys about a half mile further up. We caught up with them. The boys gave the excuse they didn't think the girls could make it, so they turned around. But the girls went on with Howard and I. By now you could only go about twenty yards and then stop and rest. We finally made it to the top, 12,395 feet. We slid most of the way back down. She had holes in her shoes the size of silver dollars and I wore out a pair of army shoes also. We met the boys that brought the girls there and, boy, was they ever mad. Oh, I forgot, the girls were Russian girls. I wouldn't climb Mt. Fuji again if they gave me a discharge because it is more work than I do around here in a month.

Your son,
Walter

Korea

Hi Folks,

We're cruising with our task force now off Korea. I wish you could see the mighty display of power that we have with us. We've got destroyers all around us as far as the eye can see, carriers launching planes, cruisers, etc. Since we often go out-alone, it's a very pleasant sight to be with all these ships.

JWB

Peacetime

Hi Mom & Dad,

I got a drill sergeant who is not human, I don't think. It's going to be real tough for the next 7 weeks. There's no heat in here either. You only get 5 minutes to eat your food and I was able to finish half my lunch today. My tendons are hurting still. I don't know how long I'll be able to last with them like this but I'm going to try and see. I don't know when I'll be allowed to make phone calls. Would like to hear from you.

Love,
Doug

World War II

My Dearest Red top,

Here I am again. The Burma Road engineers did a good job of getting this road ready for travel. The Japanese left all the bridges out to slow up the advancing army. Until yesterday, we have been moving trucks over on a flat boat and pontoon boat but the river went up so that had to stop. I hope it doesn't rain tonight because we don't have any tents of any kind.

Always love,
Vito

World War II

Dear Folks,

Maybe I can tell you some of my battle tales or sumpin. At the time they happened it was far from funny but now some of them may sound that way. Like when I crossed the river my matches got all wet but my cigarettes were dry. So I helped search about 50 German prisoners in hopes of finding some. It wasn't my job but I needed matches. Found some too. But that was about all I did find. I was doing this while Broick was being shelled.

Love,
Bud

World War II

Dear Mom,

I'm afraid the continued good news from the war fronts is going to lead many people to believe that the war is in the bag for us, and that they can begin to ease up on their war efforts and bond buying. If this does happen, the war is going to be further prolonged and countless more lives will be lost. The more our enemies weaken, the harder we must hit them. The greater our success, the greater must be our efforts, if we wish to end the war as soon as possible.

All my love,
Joe

Desert Storm

Dear Mo,

When the war starts, you will catch me there. We just received word to take one of our pre-nerve agent pills and put on our MOPP gear, our chemical protection suit. Well, the word is that we don't know if anything will happen but it's just a precaution and yes I am scared.

I don't think you will get this letter for awhile because they said if we go to war, no mail out!! We will see a lot of casualties and we will be working long hard hours but we won't be out doing any hand-to-hand combat. The reason we are carrying our weapon is because of the threat of terrorism. Just in case.

Love always,
Christy

World War II

My Darling Mugs and Ronnie,

I received just about the most wonderful birthday present I could expect. They told us that if could be ready in time, we could leave in place of the 314th. The fate of 3500 men depends on you, they say. We climbed out of bed and went to work. Talk about cold, no lights. We worked 24 hours, knocking off only to eat. Then the Personnel Officer turned to me and said, well Beeker, didn't I hear you say something about your birthday? Will this do as a present? I was so damn sleepy I couldn't hardly see, but I'm quite sure my eyes showed him my answer. My last good night by letter, dearest. The next I'll whisper in your ear. I'm coming home!!!!!!

Forever and always,
Paul

World War II

Dear Folks,

     I also got a wrist watch off one of the prisoners. It's no 17 jewel Elgin but it's no a bad one. I've wanted one for some time. We aren't supposed to take those either and that's the first thing we look for. I was just noticing a guy filling his ammo belt with cigarettes. I once saw a cartoon by Mauldin of two guys in a fire fight & when trying to get ammo out of their belt they both had all cigarettes. I saw that exact situation actually happen once. We were getting so we're hurting for ammo.

               Love,
               Lindy

World War II

Dear Mom, Dad & Kids,

When we get to Pearl, I'll have to pinch myself to see if it is really true. As Quartermaster, I am supposed to know signaling, so I have access to signal lights & voice radio. Tonight I found a guy from Cleveland and talked to him by light then switched to radio. His girl went to the same school as Joyce, so she might know her. He invited me up to visit him and said he and his girl would take Joyce and I out a few nights, so I said "Roger." I'll talk to him more as he is in our convoy.

With love,
Joe

Vietnam

Dear Kathy;

Everyone gets on everyone's nerves. Sometimes I think it would be better to be out fighting everyday. The VC tried to blow up our hotel for a second time since I've been here. The charge didn't go off this time. I really hate violence, but I've been in more violent situations since I've been here than in my whole life. I've become involved with the racial problems. Just big fist fights with white guys who just push too damn much. I have learned that if I was black, I'd be a Panther. I've really become militant. I've made about 10 Mexican-American friends and I never realized how bad they have it.

Keep the faith,
Bob

Vietnam

Hi Honey

Today is the 17th and 22 months ago today, I said "I do" to Uncle Sam. The pictures were taken by one of my buddies. I live in that tent behind me. You don't have to tell me, I know I have a button open on my fly. I have the M-16, that's the machine gun I'm holding, named. I have "Liz" written on the handle in large letters. I really depend on Liz. I also sleep with her every night. Are you jealous? I love you so much. I think of you 25 hours a day, 8 days a week. This may sound funny but I would really like to be helping Dad and Eugene clean out the chicken coup about now.

Love & Kisses,
Tom

World War II

Dear Dad and Mom,

   I might not write for a week or 2 because we are quarantined for measles now. I sure would like to get a chance at the Japanese and get it over with. The army sure would be easy in peacetime. I like the way it sure makes a fellow tough and strong. Tell Dad if he thinks his shotgun is fast, I can load and fire 24 times, that is 3 clips in a minute and with a machine gun it's a lot faster. I sure do like to shoot my rifle.

                    Bud (Killed In Action)

World War II

Dear Kitty,

I have been assigned to the Tank Destroyers now. There sure are a bunch of swell fellows in my new outfit. They took us new fellows under their wing. The other night, some fellow came over to my tent and gave me a whole box of cookies and about half a dozen chocolate bars. It doesn't seem to make any difference where you go in the army, you always find somebody from Ohio and then you don't seem far away from home at all.

Write soon,
Bill

Vietnam

Dear Family,

Today we have just come in to our base camp after having been out in the boondocks for 25 days. Our battalion is moving to a new location to pull bridge and convoy security. Instead of letting the ARVN's pull security, they're going to have to hump the boonies, pull ambushes, pull cordons & searches and have people get killed. It's about time.

Let's hope whoever becomes president does not stop the bombing in North Vietnam. Every time the bombing drops one iota, it gives Charlie more time to cross down into the southern part of South Vietnam. But then again we (America) always wear the white hat and do things the angelic way while our enemy wears the black hat and receives their plans from the devil. Why must it be so?

Your son,
Tom (Killed In Action)

World War II

Dearest Gayle,

Had a censored letter from Walt and was glad to get his new address for I had to destroy the last letter I got from Tinian. He is in the B-29s for sure and is anxious to see Tokyo from topside. I'll sure keep my fingers crossed for him all the way for I imagine flak is plenty hot over Japan. Been reading about Germany's surrender. Hope it is complete and none of these guerrilla bands for they can give a lot of trouble for a long time. Wonder if Hitler is dead? I doubt if he had guts enough to face the music. Are the celebrations big at home? We hope not, for we want them all to remember we are still out here.

All my love,
Bob

Vietnam

Dear Julie,

Right now I'm on Day Guard until 1200. Then I can go to sleep. That's one thing you never get used to or get enough of and that's sleep. Besides it makes the time go by faster. Boy! You should see the sun rising over the ocean right now. It's really a beautiful sight. It's good to see the sun rise every morning because you know you've made it through the worst part of the night. Soon I can come home, look out and see a street instead of perimeter lights and all kinds of defensive wire. And be free to go any place I want to go.

I love you,
Gary

Theme...
BATTLE / COURAGE / FEAR

"They are meeting the challenge with exceptional skill, courage and dedication. I am proud to be with them."

Vietnam

PRESS RELEASE - 196th Light Infantry
Brigade TAY NINH, Vietnam Company B,
commanded by Captain Joseph Czuberki (He's
OK in the field, he knows his stuff) was
sweeping south when it came under heavy
sniper fire. (this sniper hit a good buddy but
he's back in the States now) The company
quickly returned fire, (we burned up about
2000 rounds on those snipers from our platoon
alone.) killing one sniper (my squad leader
killed the one) and wounding another. The
wounded VC limped away to a nearby tunnel.
A member of the brigade's "Tunnel Rat" team
(Our tunnel rat is from New Paris, Ohio. His
name is Jim Klink) entered the sniper hole,
finding only a blood-stained trail. (Our
company was the only one in the battalion that
did its job right & good.)

> Notes by:
> Robert (Killed In Action)

Vietnam

Dear Dad,

Three days ago, our company was mortared. Received a ground grenade attack on our north side and scattered small arms fire. The third platoon leader was killed, the first platoon leader wounded and eighteen others were evacuated. I didn't get a scratch, but I have never been so scared in all my life. Dad, I saw the sunrise that morning and, along with others, sat for hours in disbelief. I must have thanked the Lord a hundred times since for that sunrise.

We headed back. I saw my point man go down. When I got to him he was unconscious, shot through the chest and back. I slapped his face and told him to wake up, this was no time to be sleepin' on the job. He came to, in pain but OK. My RTO did a fine job calling in support. After going through that and seeing how all of these "scared" men become strong, good fighters, you know I can't help but respect their courage. I can't help but love them.

Keep in touch,
Bud

Korea

Hello All,

      I hope your blackberries turn out better than Mom's. She said the whole works dried up. Boy, I sure could go for a blackberry pie. I have to finish this letter. We just got a radio message that a carrying party was bringing 2 wounded men off the hill in front of us. Yesterday they brought 4 dead fellows down. One was still holding his rifle. This whole place of Korea is not a pretty place to see.

      Your old pal,
      Doe Jiggs

Vietnam

Dear Carol, Bob, Kids,

Looks like Christmas is almost here. The majority of the brigade is out on operations, so for them there won't be any Christmas or New Years but I guess that's war. We had a memorial service for SP/5 Jack Clemmons. His ship landed on the LZ to evacuate a wounded man. Jack jumped out to give a hand in bringing him to the ship. As he reached the man, a machine gun opened up and Jack was killed instantly. He left behind a wife and 3 kids. He was the first man in our company to kill a VC and the first to be killed. 39 days, "SORRY ABOUT THAT"

Love,
Lewis

World War II

Dear folks,

My first time on night guard in an outpost, I could see men moving up on us. I saw one man pointing a gun at me. Then it came, artillery in close, coming closer and closer. The man pointing the gun never went down. I found out the next day it was a fence post with a board nailed on.

That was the night I learned how to tell by the sound of a shell how & where it will land. With artillery shells you have plenty of time to take cover. With a mortar, it's whee-bang, with artillery it's wheeeeeeeee-bang. Mortar is heard a split sec. before it hits. Many a man was killed by mortar for that reason. But during an attack, both mortar and artillery is falling. In that case, all you can do is ask God for guidance and keep moving ahead. That way, most falls to your rear.

In battle, a man is an ostrich. I once hid behind a little bush and felt as safe as I do now. A bush means as much to an 88 as a grape being crushed between your fingers. That's another funny thing of war, now. Then it was far from funny.

Love,
Bud

World War II

Dear Mom and Dad,

Mom, you said something about two guys quitting on that other guy's crew. Sure, you can quit anytime you want, there's some red tape out there you can just refuse to fly. But what's the use? If everyone quit, well this war might go on for a long time and it's got to be done. I've been scared, just like everyone else, plenty of times, but I figure what's to happen will happen. If the good Lord's with you, you'll be OK.

Love,
Bud

World War II

Dear Mother, Dad and Lavonne:

When we made the landing in small boats, the water was very rough. And the boats went up and down, up and down. And it was some time before the rendezvous was complete and the wave headed for the beach. But I didn't get sick. Too scared I guess.

Love to all,
Wendell

Desert Storm

Hi Mother,

By now you know we are bombing like crazy. It was something. The Stealth was the first in, to take out the radar so the other jets could come in we had the most vital targets. The pilots told us the radar didn't even pick them up. Iraq didn't start firing until the first bomb was dropped. So, for everyone that thought the Stealth didn't work WRONG. Tonight our targets are ones the F-16 been trying to take out but can't. So who did they call, the Iraq Busters. Tell Robbie I wrote his name on one of the bombs.

All my love,
Jerry

Korea

Hello Everybody,

I thought I would spend my sleepless time writing you. People at home might think this is all over with, but they've got another think coming. It seems that people no sooner raise their children, they have to go over in somebody else's land and play cops and robbers. As they say, "there'll be Hell on earth and happiness in Heaven." Everyone gets to thinking that way when they're in a position like this.

There's a valley, called Hell's Kitchen, about 8 miles in the hills and these convoys always get ambushed. They told us there wouldn't be any guerillas in them Thar hills but there was. When them people started dropping grenades on us, we just grabbed our weapon and ammo and jump out of the trucks and dug a hole until we could see them to fire at. Boy they sure got good camouflage. When I hit one of their men, right there in the middle of combat these Communist North Koreans dragged their killed soldiers and dig a hole and bury them.

Well, I don't want to talk any more about that. Some good news: We aren't surrounded any more.

Your loving son,
Walter

World War II

Dear Mom,

    I thought I would tell you some of my experiences since I have been in Mindanao. We moved about 6 miles west of Degos up in some mountains. Here is where I came near being in the next world. The shells started falling and I hit my foxhole and I mean hit it. One would go over and the next would hit 50 yards or so closer. I imagine 10 had fallen when I got out of my foxhole and jumped in a trench the Japanese had dug. The barrage stopped. I got out of the trench and went back to my hole and there lay a piece of jagged shrapnel laying where I had been laying.

    We moved about 100 yards from that spot and dug in again. One night some Japanese slipped in and blew the school house to the next country. I had a Browning Automatic Rifle. There was a small banana grove out in front of us. Someone saw some enemy so I dumped a magazine of ammo in the spot.

    I had some clothes hanging up drying and when I looked at them the next morning, they had about ten bullet holes in them.

    Love,
    Bub

Vietnam

Dear Dad,

I've been taking patrols out day and night now. Yesterday I brought in one VC suspect. One patrol got hit the night before last and the commander tried to get arty. When they wouldn't drop any in he said he was going to surrender to the VC All he needed was a white flag and he was looking for that. Needless to say, he got his arty. I've been studying up on stuff like calling in arty, med evacs, patrolling, etc., because the lives of my men depend on it.

Write soon,
Bill

Theme...
        WAR DAMAGE
        (Ravages of War)

"I never want to experience again what I have in the past two months. Hope to get home sometime soon."

Vietnam

Dear Carol, Doug & Karin & Shelly,

   I came here with two reasons. One is to get out of here alive, the other was for a Combat Infantryman Badge. I've already got that. You get it for either 30 days in the field or making contact with the enemy so I won it both ways. When I get home, I'll wear it proud. I don't think I'll ever be able to tell you if I think we belong here because I still haven't made up my mind.

                    Love you all,
                    Jim (Killed In Action)

World War II

My Dearest Wife and Son,

I have seen one of the worst atrocities than I thought humanly possible. Last Friday, there were 1100 Russian and French prisoners, possibly one American, in a little town. The Germans knew we were coming and they had to move quick. They had these men dig two huge deep graves for themselves. But we came too fast for them and they had to act quicker so they crammed these men into a little brick barn and spread straw all around and saturated it with gasoline, locked the steel doors and set fire to the place and those men burned to death in that trap. Those along the walls and around the doors tried to beat holes in the brick with their bare hands, believe it or not managed to make small holes in them. Some tunneled under the doors and those who did get out were met with machine gun fire.

Honest honey, it was the awfulest sight I have ever seen. One day while I was up with the company I did something that has been bothering me ever since, even to the point of dreaming about it and it has really haunted me. Now, since seeing this, I don't feel as bad about it at all.

All My Love Forever,
Paul

Vietnam

Dear Folks,

First let me tell ya I'm alright, so don't have hysterics. I'm in the hospital. I stepped on a booby trap April 15. It sent a bullet through my left calf. I shattered the bone but I kept tellin the Doc not to cut it off. He did a great job. Yesterday, a Captain and a SP/4 came in and presented me with the Purple Heart right in the ward. They pinned it to my pillow where everybody could see it. It brought a tear to my eye.

Take care, God bless,
pray for me.
Steve

World War II

R. FRANK HANNEMAN THE SECRETARY OF WAR DESIRES THAT I TENDER HIS DEEP SYMPATHY TO YOU IN THE LOSS OF YOUR SON STAFF SERGEANT IGNATIUS W. (DELETED) WHO WAS PREVIOUSLY REPORTED MISSING IN ACTION. REPORT NOW STATES HE WAS KILLED IN ACTION TWENTY FIRST FEBRUARY IN GERMANY. CONFIRMING LETTER FOLLOWS.

J A ULIO
THE ADJUTANT GENERAL

World War II

Dear Folks,

Concerning that Atomic Bomb. I really believe that Man has invented such a thing and even though it may have ended the war quickly, I can't bring myself to believe it's a good thing. To me it spells the destruction of everything. We call the Germans and Japanese murderers because they bombed open cities. Well with that we are certainly not much better. We have not been quite as righteous in all this as we are led to believe. Don't get the idea that I'm a convert Nazi or anything like that. I just think this whole thing is a mess and I'm not sure the proper steps are being taken to prevent more. We're still looking out mostly for ourselves.

Love,
Bob

World War II

Dear Jean,

     I never saw such pitiful sights in all my life. The natives, most of them are highly civilized, were dressed in rags but the part that amazed me was the fact that everything they wore was spotless. I noticed that some of them even had on starched shirts even though they were ragged. The men looked half starved but the women were the ones my heart went out to. Some of the women were carrying little children, part Japanese and part Filipino. This is the truth. If only the folks back home could see how the enemy has wrecked the lives of these innocent people.

     Love,
     LeRoy

World War II

Dear Family,

Our biggest scare was from one of our own planes crashing on the field. Because of bad weather, our planes had to return with their bombs. As they were circling the field and peeling off for their landings, two planes collided in the air. None of the crews had a chance to jump as they weren't very high. One plane crashed about 100 feet in front of our Ord shop. As it hit the ground, one five hundred pound bomb blew up. We all hit the dirt, which just comes natural at a time like this. A person doesn't realize how great an explosion bombs make. There were twenty men killed in this incident.

With love,
Phill

World War II

My Darling Wife:

Love and thanks to the sweetest mother on earth this Mother's day. Photos of Tom and Patsy received. Red Cross packages arrived and individual parcels delivered daily so I hope to receive yours soon. Harry Truman of Independence can help you with the following: I authorize you to draw from my balance with the finance officer, United States Army at Washington, District of Columbia, partial pay in the sum of $2500 to be used for the support of my family.

Love,
Michael (POW)

Vietnam

Dear Mom & Dad,

Sorry that I have not been able to write but this Purple Heart cost me a little bit more blood than the previous two! My right shoulder is broken and hand and arm injured so I'm writing this left handed. I'm in great spirits, so please don't worry!

Love, your son,
Freddie

World War II

Dearest Effie,

Yes, I would rather be home telling my experiences than anything else in the world but it will just have to wait. We have forgot all the little details and I'm glad we can forget some of the sights. Some experiences will always stick because I was scared so bad some nights I never expected to see the light again.

With loads of love & kisses,
Your Floyd

World War II

Dearest Louise,

     I am still alive. I guess I have lost all of my other things that I ever owned. We had a little trouble over a target and I had to bail out of the plane. Some of my crew will never be back though.
     I never want to experience again what I have in the past two months. Hope to get home sometime soon.

       Love,
       Dick

Theme...
CHRISTMAS

*"Christmas eve, and
as usual I am thinking
of home"*

World War II

Dear Sis & Family,

Christmas eve, and as usual I am thinking of home. How I would like to be in any old place in the States right now. Last Christmas I was on the train and this one here. Hope my next one will be at home. When we have a spare minute we spend it trying to get warm. Our mud is all frozen now so can't complain of the mud any more. Tomorrow is Christmas Day. Just another war work day, except for the turkey. I guess you never ate a turkey cooked in an army field kitchen (?) did you? Merry Christmas to you and yours. With lots of love to everyone.

Your brother,
Delbert (Killed In Action)

Vietnam

Dear Dawn,

Merry Christmas, Babe. I know that you will get this a long time after Christmas, so I'll wish you a Happy New Year, too. I was very proud of you when I heard your voice on the tape. I was also very happy to hear you sing, "I Wish You a Merry Christmas" because it was the night before Christmas when I got it, and it was just right!

I am putting in something special for your tooth and because Mommy said you were being so good, making your bed and hanging up your coat. I hope you are still doing it.

Love,
Donald

Vietnam

Dearest Kathie,

Hello Love! Dig it, it's Christmas. I don't feel like writing today, I'm a little depressed. This day is a total lose to me. I've got to get ready for an ambush pretty soon anyway. We've got some beer but I haven't had any and I don't want any. I've got to go. I love you.

With all my love,
Thom

World War II

Dear Mother,

By the time this letter reaches you I suppose it won't be more than a few days until Christmas so I'll send my best wishes for a very Merry Christmas. There is little need to say that I would like to be there with all of you. From the way everything looks I think I will be next year. Circumstances could be so much worse than they are and I think both of us know that. All of us have our health and that is just about everything. When one stops to think of how others have fared out of this war, we should be a bit ashamed. You might say all we have had is a bit of inconvenience and that's all. I didn't mean to make a sermon of this, but I want to let you know just how I feel about it.

Love,
Edward

Vietnam

Papa, Mommy, Hugh, Mary, Sally and
Stephanie,

Mong Le Giang Sinh, Best Wishes

- FOR A VERY MERRY CHRISTMAS
    AND A HAPPY NEW YEAR

Possibly your most unusual Christmas card

Joe

Peacetime

Dear Family,

The sea has been very smooth the last 3 or 4 days. I hope everyone is fine and I say again don't bother about Christmas presents, really, for they probably wouldn't get here anyway.

Love,
Joe

World War II

Dearest Sis,

    Hello, Sis, Leo and I will be thinking of you this Christmas, and we will be looking at the same old moon and sky and there will be a prayer in our hearts the same as there will be in yours, and I feel sure that we will be together next Christmas. This sure is a cockeyed world, isn't it Sis?

        Love,
        Bruce

Vietnam

Hi, Tiger,

I saw the pictures Mommy sent. That's a pretty tree you have this year. Did you and Donna help Mommy decorate it? You three did a very good job. Daddy couldn't have done any better. I'll let you three do it next year too. OK? Remember to be good for me. I love you so much and miss you a bunch. Hope Santa was good to you.

Love,
Daddy

Korea

Seasons Greetings from First Marine Division

Dearest Authorine,

I will be with you in thought on Christmas and will remember you in my prayers. May you have a very merry and joyous Christmas and my God bless you on that day.

All my love always,
Tom

World War II

MARINE BARRACKS PARRIS ISLAND, S.C.
25 DECEMBER 1941
CHRISTMAS MENU

Shrimp Cocktail
Green Olives
Stuffed Celery - Mixed Sweet Pickles
Roast Young Turkey
Virginia Baked Ham
Savory Bread Dressing
Snow Flake Potatoes - Giblet Gravy
Cranberry Sauce
Asparagas Tips
Marshmallow Sweet Potatoes
Fruit Cake - Mince Pie
Ice Cream
Hot Rolls - Bread - Butter.
Mixed Nut - Fresh Fruit
Coffee

E.P. Moses Brigadier General, U.S. Marine
Corps Commanding General
        submitted by:
        PVT Albert Huff, USMC

Theme...
FOREIGN CULTURE

"If you don't have any money, you are burned with dried cow dung"

World War II

Dear Mrs. Connolly,

I wish more people would ask questions in their letters so I would have something to write about. The natives with any connections at all with the soldiers do take to US ways. Money doesn't mean much to the soldiers, and the natives know it. A ride in a rickshaw costs us about ten times as much as it would for a native. A rupee note is worth some 33 cents and it takes a year to realize it isn't just a cigar coupon, even if it does look like one.

I think the natives eat the same thing, and that is rice. Of course, if they get a little more money, then they can buy a goat, which is about the only kind of meat they eat. But I remember one time one of the fellows killed a lizard about four feet long and gave it to some natives to skin for him. The natives ate the lizard.

When a native dies, he is cremated before sundown. He is put on a bed and carried to the burning Ghats. If you don't have any money, you are burned with dried cow dung, but if you do, you get a nice wood fire. It takes about five hours. Then your ashes are thrown in the sacred river.

As ever,
Jim

World War II

Dear Mother and Dad,

We have an animal here for a pet. It's the cutest thing I've seen. It's called a Wombat. It's a cross between, or at least it looks like, a variety of animals. It has a head like a possum, eyes like a raccoon, hands, feet and tail like a monkey and a pouch like a kangaroo. It's hands and feet are like humans. They have finger and toe nails and lines in the palms of his hands. It's guise a sight. Maybe I can get a picture of him.

Theodore

World War II

Dear Folks,

We are camped in a coconut grove so we have to be careful of the nuts. A direct hit could cause plenty of damage. I saw a big naval battle the other morning. It kept me awake for some time. Japanese planes go over every day. The natives here are very friendly, clean, intelligent and nice looking but much in need of clothing. Of course, we don't have many ourselves just at present. For clothes, they exchange chickens, eggs, bananas and potatoes and some kind of drink called Tuba, so some such name. I found out the other day that the word "Ohio" means good morning in Japanese. I have the word on my hat and one of the natives told me about it.

Love,
Charles

Vietnam

Dear Mom, Dad, Greg and Kenneth,

Tell dad if he would pay the shipping charges, I'll send him a water buffalo. Everybody ought to have one. Ha. It's really funny you will see these old Mama-Sans out in the field. plowing with them and there will be a little baby laying on their back asleep. As soon as I get a camera, I'll get some pictures of it. But tell dad he don't know what he is missing unless he has two water buffalos to plow his fields with.

Terry

World War II

Dear Mom & Family,

    We had a big snow storm this afternoon. I was talking to an English fellow the other day, he said since the Yanks came to this country, the living has changed, the women have changed and now he thinks the weather is changing. He said this was more snow than he had seen in a long time. I told him that he ought to see some of the ones we have at home.

      Love,
      Earl

Vietnam

Hi Andy,

Our home is in a rubber tree area. The trees look like a carpet from the air and are in rows. I saw a Montagnard woman in downtown Song Be who had nice black PJ bottoms on but no top. Just like National Geographic. Eat your vitamins, I do. Mind Mom and be nice to Math.

Sending love,
Dad

Vietnam

Dearest Deb,

On the way to the PX today, we saw a little girl who was either hit by a truck or fell off it while it was moving. She was all banged up and was bleeding bad from the back of her head. I felt so sorry for her. She was only about four years old. We got her to a Vietnamese hospital and when I carried her in the stupid people just looked at me. Here I was with a kid covered with blood and hurt and these people just looked at me. Well, finally she got taken care of. I hope she's not hurt too bad. I guess I have a soft spot for kids. I hate to see one hurt.

Love ya,
Eric

Vietnam

Dear Grandparents,

We have seen a few elephants and very many water buffalo. This country is generally pretty flat, in this particular area, anyway. There are a few mountains, they seem to be scattered all around. The better part of the land is covered by jungle, then there are rice paddies and very many old plantations from the French. I don't know the whole thing, but I do understand the French tried to take over the country. Their railroads and logging roads are still here, but they're pretty much grown over. Their old rubber plantations are really beautiful, though. They've taken large areas of land and spaced the trees. Now the trees are really tall and they cut out the light so there is very little brush below. The people make bread in mud huts and it's really good.

Yours truly,
Joe

Vietnam

Dear Robbie,

I had to get a driver's license over here since I'm in charge of the LT's jeep. When I took the test, I not only had to know the speed limits in miles but I also had to know them in kilometers which is what the Vietnamese use. Also, I had to take a sign test. Since I can't read Vietnamese or French, I had to memorize what the signs looked like. We don't use regular money here. Instead, we use Military Payment Certificates, which is special money for US servicemen in foreign countries. When we buy things from the Vietnamese, we have to use their money, called plasters.

Mike

Vietnam

Dear Jackson, Ohio:

When departing from Tan Son Nhut, a GI
is automatically and unceremoniously set upon
by hordes of cyclo drivers. This cat is wearing a
pair of cracked Foster Grants, greasy khakis, a
black-T shirt that used to be white and a green
Army fatigue shirt with the name "Jurgensonn"
on it. We got into the stream of traffic and floated
right on down the boulevard like a rubber canoe
in rapids. He must have skipped a lot of school
'cause he didn't read all those stop signs. Those
sunglasses must have been really dark, 'cause we
didn't stop for any of those red lights. Must have
been exciting to watch, but I had my eyes closed,
so I missed it. Miracle of miracles, we got there in
one piece. Already he had his hand on his chin,
looking up, in deep thought calculating the fare.
He announces grandly, "five hunda pi." I
directed a few derogatory Vietnamese words at
him. No way it cost that much. We negotiated. I
gave him half of his new price. He directed a few
derogatory American words at me and tried to
run me down. I escaped, only to fight another
day against the cyclos of Saigon.

L. White

Theme...
PATRIOTISM

*"There were tears in our
eyes when they raised
the American flag in our
prison camp."*

Vietnam

Hello My Dearest,

As I think of it, Americans tend to think of freedom and democracy as being the same. This is not so as I think of it. One can be free and live under a form of government other than ours. It would seem that this is a part of the problem. We feel a certain group of people won't be happy until we give them a democratic form of government. Actually, I want to use what talent and energy I have toward helping rather than hurting. You know, my love, I don't believe I'll ever retire from a useful endeavor.

Much love,
Joseph (Killed In Action)

Vietnam

Dear Dad,

We haven't been able to find the NVA. He's been awfully quiet. I think something is going to happen soon. It's like instinct to everyone. Guys are cleaning their weapons every spare min.

Dad, if anything happens, please remember I am not bitter towards the army or the war. If anything us guys are disgusted at the blind hypocrites who are more worried about how much they can cheat on income taxes or how much of a military genius they are. They can solve the war by sitting at home drinking cold beer in a soft chair watching TV. They say the government and army are just wasting the money while downing 5 or 6 $2.50 drinks. But this is as far as they go, just criticism. They don't know a damn thing about the realistic problem. They ignore the fact that thousands of young men have sacrificed their lives & others have given limbs or eyes or have been mutilated just so the protesters can go on protesting and blowing their minds on drugs and so self-appointed experts on world affairs can get fatter and richer while feeling smug and pleased with themselves. They haven't seen a people starving to

death in a nation that's been fighting for hundreds
of years to get what the ugly American takes for
granted, so lightly. They also haven't seen these
same people homeless & childless after a mortar
attack. May God help the empty black-hearted
people who are like this on Judgement Day.

Love & Miss All,
Jan

Vietnam

Dear Mom,

      I just got over a bout with a bug. However, this war didn't stop because the Cav was sick. We took some pretty big losses in-the A Shau Valley. The first day, we lost 7 Hueys, 2 gun ships, 2 Chinooks and one flying crane. 7 crew members killed, 10 injured. If a ship went down, the next aircraft went in to pick up the crew, regardless of the ground fire.

      This is the same age group as the majority of the "peace" demonstrators and draft card burners in the States. In a way, Mom, I wish you could have seen it as it was enough to restore your faith in American youth. It doesn't take any courage to sit in & say they won't go to war, they won't fight, LBJ is a murderer, etc. These young men over here were scared also, knowing the next round might get them, but they did it, time and time again because someone has to pay the price for our freedoms in the States & the free world. I'm proud to be a member of the 1st Cav Div and proud to be an American. I wonder how many draft dodgers can say they are proud to be Americans.

                Your son,
                Bill

Desert Storm

Mom, Dad, Becky and Miracle,

I'm not going to lie to you and say I'm not scared, because I am. I'm dug in a real fortified foxhole and am loaded up with enough firepower. I feel safe cause all the explosives, weapons and rocket launchers I have and I can operate them all perfectly. I sure am grateful I have 4 ½ years experience. I look at some of the privates around me and I can sense the uncertainty in them.

I sure feel sorry for the first person I see burning a flag when I get home! We hear news about all the anti-war protests going on in the states. I wish I could bring some of them over here. They just don't realize how many men and women are over here risking their lives for the country they're protesting against.

I can't talk about a lot of the missions I've been on. But you can be sure that the boys in Vietnam and Korea had it a lot worse than me.

Love you all,
Yogi

World War II

Dearest June Louise,

Most of the officers and men in my squadron took the news of Roosevelt's death with silence. He meant so much to each of us that considerable readjustment was necessary. His death was a great personal loss. What comments there were conjectured the abilities of Harry S. Truman. His humbleness and forthright outspokenness soon won him wholehearted support.

All of us knew that our ally, Russia, would not be excluded from any armistice agreement. Those of us fighting the war out here realize the importance of making and keeping friends. No one is more anxious to get the war over than we are, but we don't want to win the war and lose the peace again. Victory should be signal for sober reflection on the responsibility of world leadership toward peace. Americans should begin to realize their power and prestige. The fighting man knows it. It's time the people at home learned it.

Love and kisses,
Jim

World War II

Dear Mom and Dad,

There is a noticeable stillness in the barracks tonight. We were restricted of all liberty this evening. All the fellows are checking their equipment and writing last minute letters to their wives, parents or friends. There is the usual racket by the ones who have come back, the battle wise Marines who have done a job in the Pacific that will live forever. We are all green, but confident of the task which awaits us, and we will fulfill that job which will seal the doom of the now setting sun of Japan. They will be thrown back and thrown back, beaten again and again until we have crushed the last bit of living resistance and we have the Stars and Stripes flying over Tokyo. How we're looking forward to the day when the last shot is fired, when the slaughter of innocent people who never wanted this war will cease and they can breathe the air of freedom once again. I don't know where we'll strike, but whenever and wherever it is, God help them.

Lots of love always,
Walt

World War II

Dear Mom and Dad,

It's over! Yippee! I'm in London on a three day pass and enjoying V-J Day but in a quiet way. I didn't know that there was so many people in the world as I saw on Piccadilly Square last night. Us GI Joes who fought in the war and who had a good reason for being gay was standing on the curb watching the civilians and wondering what all the excitement was about. The average fellow just said, "well it's over and done with, now let's go home." I don't feel excited yet, rather just a deep thankfulness. Columbus is what I want to see.

Dolly

World War II

Dear Mom and Dad,

Sorry for not writing in such a long time but the Germans didn't let us write very many letters, so I sent them all to Ruth. I haven't heard from Ruth since October, I never received any letters while in prison. I pray to God that she is alright! I would like to been there when the baby came, but I just can't get there in time I am leaving France tomorrow.

The Germans didn't treat us very well but we knew the war couldn't last forever and sooner or later we would be free again. There were tears in our eyes when they raised the American flag in our prison camp.

Your loving son,
Waren

Korea

My Darlings Nancy and Donna,

Believe me when I say you're lucky to be born in America. Our country probably isn't running as smooth as I would like to see it but it could be much worse as you would learn should you have been born to someone else in a different land. As you grow up place your trust in God and go to church as often as you can. Pray for your daddy and if everything goes alright, I'll be home to take you and Mommy to church every Sunday. Should anything happen to me, please remember my only thoughts were of you.

All my love forever,
Daddy

Theme...
FAMILY

"I am awfully proud when I show the fellows you and Sandy's pictures and say, that's my wife and daughter"

Vietnam

Dear Jackleen,

This is destined to be a sad letter because that is how I'm feeling. I promise this will be the only sad letter you receive. I know we promised faithfully never to write a letter like this. Indulge me this once. Do you realize how much those last several days together meant to me? then you know how much the last seven years have meant. How lonely my life would have been had it not been for you. When I think back, I feel that we must have lived two lifetimes worth and I would gladly live two more. The prospect of spending a year separated from you leaves me numb. I am consoled by the thought that you are living as normal an existence as possible. I pray that you are. I have spent all these lines telling you how sad I am and now I say you shouldn't be. These thoughts will not be repeated. I will learn to live with them tucked away. Occasionally I will call one forth, savor it for awhile and tuck it away again.

Did you see me as I waved goodbye to your airplane? I was standing on the car but you probably were on the other side of the plane.

All my love,
King Edward IV
(Killed In Action)

Vietnam

Hi Honey,

I did my wash and have been laying around talking and thinking of you & home. I just can't find the right words to say how much I miss you and need you. You're the most important thing in my life and I can't take being away from you. I was so sad and lonely last night and maybe that's why I got so drunk so I could come back and go to sleep without thinking about it. I just tried to fill up that big empty space with a bottle. It worked for a while, but now I feel worse than ever. Everybody is in the same boat. Guys I've only known for a while I can talk to real well. They know what I'm talking about.

All my love,
Bob (Killed In Action)

Vietnam

Hi Hon,

Well this marks 6 months in Vietnam. I wish I was coming home tomorrow. Why don't you write me and tell me what you have planned for that first night and I'll see if it's about the same thing I have planned, OK? I got your package the day before my birthday and Mom's and my sisters' packages. I don't think I have to tell you which package I enjoyed the most because you know just what little goodies your hubby enjoys. I know this don't have anything to do with what I was writing before but all of a sudden I got tears in my eyes just because of some music on the radio. You probably guessed it the theme from "Love Story." Brenda, I ain't kidding, I want to be with you so bad right now I just hurt all over inside. I feel like just starting to scream and not stopping until they put me on a plane to bring me back to you.

Love,
Larry

World War II

My Dearest, Darling Wife,

I love you my darling, more than anything in the world. Sweetheart, I will always love you and honor you, for you are the finest, dearest, sweetest wife in the world. I miss you with all my heart, dearest. You are in all of my thoughts and dreams forever, my dear Mrs. Cooper.

I am thousands of miles away in the middle of a war, yet each evening my thoughts go back to you and Davie, to our future life together and to that pretty little home we will have.

The weather here is just rain and more rain every day. I wear a camouflaged jungle uniform I call my jungle zoot suit. I will close now and write you again tomorrow night. Forever and ever.

PS It is almost time for our nine o'clock date. I kissed your picture. Goodnight darling.

Alfred

World War II

Hi Son,

   Daddy was laying here thinking about you and since you have a birthday coming I thought that you should rate a letter. A letter is about all daddy can give you for your birthday this year, but maybe next year I will be able to get you a nice present. Will that be alright? I would buy you something over here and send it to you but where I am at now, and have been, there just isn't anything to buy. The Germans took everything with them when they left. Do you know where daddy is now? I bet you don't. How have you been getting alone lately? Daddy hasn't heard from you or mommy in a long time. Have you been a good boy? Do you mind mommy and do what she tells you? Do you and poppy still have your ups and downs? I bet you don't even know how old you are, do you? Have you been up to see Theresa's new sister lately? By the way, how much do you like your daddy? Have you

been saying your prayers every night? Daddy
says goodnight to you and mommy every
night. Well honey I guess I'll close this letter by
wishing you: A VERY, VERY HAPPY
BIRTHDAY.

Your Daddy
(Killed In Action) 3-29-45

World War II

Darling,

You women are always ready to believe the worst about the French women! I personally do not believe that they are any worse than the girls in America. They may have different ideas about morals but to me there is little distinction as to whether you do it openly or secretly. You accomplish the same purpose either way. Don't accuse me of speaking from experience because I am just an observant soul. French girls are either awfully good or awfully bad. I know too, that a broad-minded wife to send me shoes to give to these "immoral" French. I hope this trust will produce the shoes!

I love you darling,
Tommy

World War II

Hello Darling,

Should anything happen to me, you'll get $105.10. In the event you ever decide to remarry, you will continue to draw $55.10 a month for 240 months. Together with my civilian policy, you will be all set, my darling. Of course, I am going to be selfish and hope that you won't remarry. You really couldn't expect anything else of me. What's more, sweet darling. I am coming back. I just got to, to a sweet wife like you. I just wanted to let you know what is what in the event God decides I am not to come back.

Your loving Bill

World War II

My Darling Red top,

Today they played a rebroadcast of the Spot Light Hit Parade from Patterson Field, Ohio and that was all I needed to make me wish I was back home with my Darling. They played, "There Go That Song Again" and I was wondering-if they would play our song and they seem to answer my thought cause they played it. My memories went back again to you as Always with the song by the same name. Baby, my love for you will be Always and the only way it will ever change is that it will become greater as it is by the minute.

Always love,
Vito

World War II

My Darlings Pudge & Sandy,

    I got the pictures and, gee, Darling, those of Sandy are sure cute. She sure has the fattest little cheeks, and the prettiest smile. the two of you, Darling, are really wonderful and the Easter hat is real nice. You are sure the prettiest thing in that outfit, Honey. Is that the suit you wore when we got married? I will never forget that evening, Darling, if I live to be a thousand. You know, Honey, I am awfully proud when I show the fellows you and Sandy's pictures and say, "that's my wife and daughter." Well, Darling, goodnight for now, and dream of me.

              Yours forever,
              A1

Vietnam

Hi Honey,

Although we are a long way from one another. And many miles between us. We are still together in our hearts and minds, and most of all our thoughts. You be a good girl and don't forget to kiss my picture every night. Because some night, it might just kiss back. I love you very much and baby too.

Keep smiling Punk!
Bill/Daddy

Theme...
POLITICS

"I think too many people have the wrong idea about how this war is to be won."

World War II

Dear Mother, Dad & All,

Well, it looks as if hostilities may cease any time now but still some "heroes" are making a fight for it. The recent discoveries of atrocities sure shows how low man can get when he leaves God out of his life. How utterly ruthless these people are. The only way I can see to keep them under control is rigid policing which will have to carried on for generations. Yes, my children, if God so grants my desires, I will do some of this policing. No one knows or can calculate how many years we the people have been set back. If people ever forget the price of this holocaust then truly human beings are dupes. God has sure purged the world for greed of money and power.

Love,
Jim

Vietnam

Dear Uncle Vince, Aunt Adriana and family,

I think too many people have the wrong idea about how this war is to be won. It has to be won not only with bullets but also with kindness and good will. The main objective, I think, over here, should be to try to win the hearts and minds of the people and make them realize that the government the Communists are trying to force on them is no good. But all we can do is play along and hope that some day there will be an end to all this. I am sure of one thing, though. From the state of things over here now, peace is nowhere in the near future.

Love,
Bill

Vietnam

Dear Debbie,

Last night I watched some fighting on the mountain about 5 miles away. They were dropping flares so I could see real well. Kinda gave me a funny feeling knowing that people are getting killed out there as I watched. Now, after I've seen this place and after getting shot at here, I don't believe anyone will win this war. We could if we tried hard enough but all we're doing is playing a costly and silly game. Sooner or later we're going to be kicked out of here or else this will turn into a full war, which I hope not.

Published by: Dan Meeks & Dave Aldstadt
www.allmilitary.com
P.O. Box 10
Grove City, OH 43123-0010